THE BOOK OF....

DINOSAURS

 KINGFISHER

First published 2012 by Kingfisher
an imprint of Macmillan Children's Books
a division of Macmillan Publishers Limited
20 New Wharf Road, London N1 9RR
Basingstoke and Oxford
Associated companies throughout the world
www.panmacmillan.com

Written and illustrated by Dynamo Ltd
Concept by Jo Connor

ISBN 978-0-7534-3500-7

Copyright © Macmillan Children's Books 2012

10 9 8 7 6 5 4 3 2 1
TTR/0512/LFG/140MA

A CIP catalogue for this book is available
from the British Library.

Printed in China

WHAT'S IN THIS BOOK?

DINOSAURS...

HAVE YOU EVER WONDERED WHY... OR WHAT...OR WHEN?

It's only natural to wonder about the world around us. It's a very complicated and surprising place sometimes. And you'll never understand what is going on around you unless you ask yourself a question every now and again.

We have investigated the prehistoric world to collect as many tricky dinosaur questions as we could find...

...and we also found the answers for you!

We now invite you to come with us on our journey around the world of dinosaurs, so that we can show you all the answers we have discovered.

Did you know ...

Some dinosaur fossils are very valuable. Specimens of Archaeopteryx (ar-kee-op-terr-ix) – the very first bird – are extremely rare and worth around £10 million!

We also thought it might be fun to see how much of this shiny new knowledge you can remember – so at the back of the book, on pages 56 and 57, you'll find some Quick-Quiz questions to test you out. It's not as scary as it sounds – we promise it will be fun. (And besides, we've given you all the answers on pages 58 and 59.)

While we were searching for all those answers, we found out some other pretty interesting things, too. We wrote them all down on these panels – so you can memorize these facts and impress your friends!

Are you ready for this big adventure?

Then let's go!

WHY AREN'T THERE ANY DINOSAURS IN THE ZOO?

Did you know...

Before people knew anything about dinosaurs, they thought that the dinosaur bones they found were the bones of giants or dragons.

Dinosaurs lived many millions of years ago. The last ones became extinct (died out) about 65 million years ago. Humans have only been on Earth for around two million years, so a human h never met a living dinosaur, let alone put one in a zoo.

Did you know...

Dinosaur remains are often found in lots of separate pieces, which need fitting together like a big, prehistoric jigsaw puzzle.

HOW DO WE KNOW ABOUT DINOS?

Some dinosaur bones have survived underground, and over millions of years they have slowly turned into stone fossils. When these are discovered and excavated (carefully dug up), experts can work out what kind of creature they belonged to.

DID DINOSAURS ALL LIVE AT THE SAME TIME?

Million Years Ago   250 → 200 → 150 →

Did you know...

The first dinosaurs were small and ran around on two legs. Over time, some types of dinosaur grew much bigger and began to walk on four legs.

Dinosaurs lived on Earth for about 165 million years altogether. Over this time they evolved (gradually changed), so that different types of dinosaurs lived at different times, sometimes millions of years apart.

DO WE KNOW EVERYTHING ABOUT DINOS?

"Woof"?

There are still lots of things that we don't know for sure about dinosaurs, such as what colour they were, or what noises they made. About ten new types of dinosaur are discovered every year, though, so we are gradually learning more.

Did you know...

Someone who studies fossils is called a palaeontologist. (pal-ay-on-tol-oh-gist).

WHERE DID DINOS LIVE?

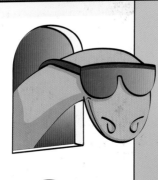

Fossils of dinosaurs have been found all over the world, but the Earth looked very different when they were alive. Since dinosaurs lived, the land on the surface of this planet has changed position and new oceans and mountains have formed.

Did you know...

Dinosaur remains have been found near the South Pole. When dinosaurs lived, it was not a frozen wasteland as it is today. The weather was much warmer, and there were lots of plants and creatures living there.

WHO WERE THE DINOS' NEIGHBOURS?

Did you know...

Dragonflies lived at the same time as the dinosaurs, but they were much bigger than they are today. Their wings stretched up to 75 centimetres wide.

Flying and swimming reptiles lived on Earth at the same time as the dinosaurs, who lived on land. There were also insects, fish and small furry mammals that looked like rats.

DID DINOSAURS EAT EACH OTHER?

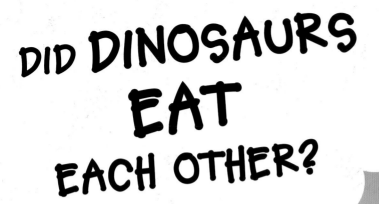

Did you know...

Some dinosaur fossils have been found with injury marks on them, where the dinosaur was bitten or slashed during a fight.

Some dinosaurs were carnivores, which means they ate meat. They hunted and ate prey (food animals). Other dinosaurs were herbivores, peaceful plant-eaters who munched on vegetation all day long. There were also a few omnivores, dinosaurs that ate both plants and meat.

HOW CAN YOU TELL IF A DINO WAS SCARY?

Predators (hunting dinosaurs) had rows of sharp teeth, strong back legs for running fast and long claws for fighting. Plant-eating dinosaurs had smaller, blunter teeth for grinding up vegetation, or sometimes a beak instead of teeth.

Did you know...

The fierce Tyrannosaurus rex (tie-ran-oh-saw-rus rex) had sharp teeth as long as bananas and a bite three times more powerful than a lion's!

WERE DINOSAURS COLOURFUL?

We do not know for sure what colour every dinosaur was. It is very rare to find fossilized dino skin, but some dinosaur remains have been found with fossilized feathers, and scientists can test these to work out what colour they were. It turns out that some of these feathers were colourful.

Did you know...

The most colourful feathered dinosaur found so far is called Anchiornis (an-kee-or-nis). It had a red head and black-and-white striped feathers on its arms and legs.

WHAT WAS DINOSAUR SKIN LIKE?

Dinosaurs were a type of animal called a reptile. Their skin was scaly and wrinkly, like modern reptiles such as crocodiles and lizards. It would have been tough, and hard to bite through.

Did you know...

Some dinosaurs had feathers. Experts think it is possible that, in certain cases, they might have evolved into birds.

WHAT DID DINOSAURS SOUND LIKE?

Did you know...

Some of the beaked dinosaurs might have made squawking noises like large modern birds, such as seagulls, do.

Dinosaurs might have made noises like modern crocodiles. Crocs make coughing, hissing and bellowing sounds when they are communicating with their family or warning off enemies.

WHICH DINOS HONKED THROUGH THEIR HEADS?

Did you know...

The hadrosaurs might have honked to each other to warn of danger, or to impress a mate. Animals do the same thing today.

Duck-billed dinosaurs, called hadrosaurs (had-row-saws), had a long, bony head crest. Inside the crest there were hollow tubes, and it is possible that the dinosaurs blew through these, using the crest like a musical instrument to make honking noises.

WERE ALL DINOSAURS HUGE?

Did you know...

The smallest dinosaurs we know about measured roughly 30 centimetres in length. These tiny creatures ran around like birds, and even had feathers.

Some dinosaurs were the biggest creatures that have ever lived on land, but others were as small as chickens. The tallest ones were plant-eaters, with very long necks for reaching high into trees. They were a group of dinosaurs called sauropods, and some of them could reach as high as a modern, five-storey building.

Did you know...

Amphicoelias would have had to eat hundreds of kilograms of plants every day, and was big enough to push whole trees over.

WHO WAS THE HEAVIEST DINO?

Tonnes

Amphicoelias (am-fee-see-lee-us) is the heaviest dinosaur we know of. It probably weighed about 100 tonnes – roughly the same as 20 African elephants. It would have shaken the ground as it walked.

DID DINOSAURS HAVE HANDS?

Dinosaurs that walked on two legs had forelimbs – short arms that ended in long fingers with claws on the end. These were not like human hands, but looked more like bird feet. The dinosaur would have used them for fighting, or for gathering food.

DID DINOSAURS HAVE TOES?

Did you know...

The biggest dinosaur footprints ever found belonged to a sauropod (sore-oh-pod). This giant plant-eater's footprints measured up to 2 metres across.

Two-legged dinosaurs had long toes with sharp claws on the end, for slashing their enemies. Four-legged dinosaurs had legs and feet more like an elephant's, with short fat toes and rounder claws.

WHO WAS THE BIGGEST HUNTER?

Did you know...

Spinosaurus could arch its back, perhaps to spread out its back fin like a giant fan.

The biggest meat-eating dinosaur we know about is Spinosaurus (spy-no-saw-rus), which grew up to 15 metres long. It had long jaws like a crocodile's and a sail-like fin down its back, which measured almost two metres high. The fin may have been for showing off, or it may have worked like a radiator to help keep the dinosaur warm or cool.

WHO HAD THE LONGEST CLAWS?

Did you know...

Some two-legged hunting dinosaurs, such as Deinonychus (dye-no-ny-cus), could flick out the claws on their feet, like flick knives. The name 'Deinonychus' means 'terrible claw'.

A two-legged, plant-eating dinosaur called Therizinosaurus (thair-ee-zine-oh-saw-rus) had three incredible, metre-long claws on each forearm, rather like curved swords. Although these claws looked vicious, the dinosaur probably used them mainly for pulling down tree branches to get at tasty leaves.

WHO WAS THE STRANGEST-LOOKING DINO?

It is hard to choose between Therizinosaurus, with its metre-long claws, shaggy coat and big fat tummy, and Incisivosaurus (in-size-iv-oh-saw-rus), a cross between a bird and a lizard, with its giant teeth sticking out of its mouth!

WHO HAD A NOISY TAIL?

The giant plant-eating dinosaur Diplodocus (dip-low-doe-cus) could swish its tail very quickly, like a whip. The tail might have made a very loud 'cracking' noise that would have scared off enemies.

COULD DINOSAURS SWIM?

Did you know...

Liopleurodon (lie-oh-ploor-oh-don) was the biggest giant reptile of the prehistoric seas. It grew up to 15 metres long, and was a terrifying hunter.

Dinosaurs were land animals, although some of them might have been able to swim short distances. If they did, they risked being eaten by the fierce swimming reptiles that lived in the oceans in prehistoric times. Some of these were as big as whales, with huge jaws and sharp teeth.

COULD
DINOSAURS FLY?

Did you know...

One of the largest pterosaurs ever found was Quetzalcoatlus (kwet-sal-co-at-lus). It had a wingspan of 11 metres – wider than a hang glider.

Dinosaurs could not fly, but pterosaurs could. They were flying reptiles that lived at the same time as the dinosaurs. They had wings made of thin skin, like a bat's wings. Their jaws were long and pointed, like beaks, and some had sharp teeth.

WHO WAS THE FASTEST DINO?

Struthiomimus (strooth-ee-oh-mime-us) had long, thin legs like an ostrich's, and it could probably run up to 80 kilometres per hour - almost as fast as a racehorse. It may have needed to run to escape its enemies.

Did you know...

Scientists have worked out how fast dinosaurs moved by measuring the spaces between their footprints. Many dinosaurs who left footprints moved no faster than a person walking.

COULD DINOSAURS
CLIMB TREES?

Some of the dinosaurs could probably climb. A feathered dinosaur called Microraptor (my-crow-rap-tor) had curved claws like a squirrel's, which might have helped it to grip branches.

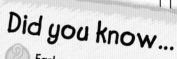

Did you know...

Early on in dinosaur times there were no grasses or flowering plants, and few trees. But gradually, over millions of years, thick forests grew over parts of the Earth.

DID DINOSAURS LIVE IN FAMILIES?

Some plant-eating dinosaurs lived in big herds, like modern animals do on the plains of Africa. Hunters might have lived together in small family groups, like wolves or lions do today.

Did you know...

We know that plant-eaters often lived in herds because they have left fossilized footprint trails, made by lots of animals moving along together.

DID DINOSAURS HAVE HOMES?

NESTING SITE

CAFE

Most dinosaurs probably did not have one particular home. They may have migrated, which means that they moved to different places at different times of the year. They did sometimes have special nesting sites, though, where the females went to lay their eggs.

WHO LAID THE BIGGEST EGGS?

A plant-eater called Hypselosaurus (hip-sell-oh-saw-rus) laid the biggest dinosaur eggs we know about. Each egg was nearly 30 centimetres long and 25 centimetres wide, about as big as 73 chicken eggs put together.

Did you know...

Hypselosaurus did not make a nest, but might have buried its eggs in sand, like a turtle does.

WHAT DID DINO NESTS LOOK LIKE?

Many dinosaurs built nests by scraping a hollow circle in the ground, with a rim of earth around it. When they had laid their eggs, they piled layers of earth or plants on top to keep them warm.

WHAT WERE DINOSAUR BABIES LIKE?

Baby dinosaurs were tiny versions of their parents. Life would have been very dangerous for them until they grew big enough to fight, or to run away from hungry hunters.

Did you know...

Baby dinosaurs chipped their way out of their eggs, just like baby birds do today.

WHICH DINOS LOOKED AFTER THEIR BABIES?

A plant-eating dinosaur called Maiasaura (my-ah-sore-ra) was a good mother. Fossilized females have been found near their babies. They were probably looking after them until they grew big enough to live on their own.

Did you know...

The name 'Maiasaura' means 'good mother lizard'. These mothers probably protected their babies from fierce predators.

HOW BIG WAS DINO POO?

Dinosaurs have left fossilized poo behind. Scientists call them 'coprolites'. The biggest one found so far was 43 centimetres long. It may have come from a Tyrannosaurus rex. Plant-eaters produced a lot of droppings, like modern cattle do.

Did you know...

Scientists can tell whether dinosaurs ate plants or meat by studying their fossilized poo.

HOW WELL COULD DINOSAURS SMELL?

Dinosaurs had big nostrils and a long muzzle (nose and mouth parts), so they probably had a good sense of smell. Meat-eaters might have had the best sense of smell though, because they had to find prey.

Did you know...

Tyrannosaurus rex had a very large muzzle, probably to sniff out its food.

DID DINOSAURS LIKE TO SUNBATHE?

Did you know...

Humans are warm-blooded, which means we can create some body heat of our own. Modern reptiles are cold-blooded. They need to get heat from the sun to keep their body warm.

People once thought that dinosaurs were cold-blooded. This means they needed the sun to help them to keep their bodies warm, like mode snakes and lizards do. Now it is thought they might have been warm-blooded, so they would have been able to live in cold places as well as warm ones.

DID DINOSAURS LIVE IN COLD PLACES?

Some dinosaurs lived in places where it was cold and dark in the winter. They might have eaten as much as they could in summer, and lived off their body fat in winter, like bears do today.

Did you know...

A dinosaur called Troodon (troo-oh-don) lived in the far north of the world. It had feathers to keep it warm, and big eyes that helped it to hunt in the dark, like a modern owl does.

DID DINOSAURS WEAR ARMOUR?

Some dinosaurs had very tough, bony plates on their body, like armour. Some had spikes and horns, too, to defend themselves from hungry attackers.

Did you know...

Ankylosaurus (an-ky-low-saw-rus) was like a dino tank! It had armour-plated skin, spikes and horns, and a big club on the end of its tail, like a giant hammer.

WHO WAS THE SPIKIEST DINO?

Did you know...

It's possible that dinosaurs with long neck spikes could clatter them together to make a frightening noise.

A plant-eater called Edmontonia (ed-mon-toe-nee-ah) had the most spikes. They were on its neck, shoulders and sides. It might have charged like a rhino when it was threatened by enemies.

DID DINOS HAVE GOOD EYESIGHT?

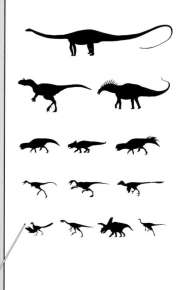

Dinosaurs probably had good eyesight to help them hunt for food. But nobody knows what colour their eyes were, or if the irises (the black centres of the eyes) narrowed to slits in bright light, like a cat's eyes do.

Did you know...

Troodon had the biggest dino eyes we know about. They were 4.5 centimetres wide, about the same size as an ostrich's eye.

COULD DINOSAURS SEE IN THE DARK?

Some dinosaurs had night vision. The Velociraptor (vee-loss-ee-rap-tor), a vicious hunting dinosaur, might have been a night-time hunter. To stay safe, plant-eaters may have rested in herds, taking short naps where others were awake and could warn of night-time danger.

WERE DINOSAURS THIEVES?

Did you know...

Some dinosaurs nested in big groups, like seabirds do, which made it easier for them to defend their eggs and babies from hungry enemies on the prowl.

Some dinosaurs probably stole and ate the eggs of other dinosaurs. Birds and lizards steal eggs in a similar way today.

Did you know...

Stegosaurus's back plates might have been brightly coloured to attract other Stegosauruses.

Lots of dinosaurs had body parts that were probably for showing off to attract mates. Some had head crests, sails or big plates on their backs. A dinosaur called Stegosaurus (steg-oh-saw-rus) had the biggest back plates, sticking up at least 70 centimetres high.

HOW WERE DINOSAUR FOSSILS MADE?

Dinosaur bones could become fossiliz[ed] if they were buried under layers of sand or mud, perhaps in a lake or rive[r] many millions of years ago. Over time the bones would gradually harden o[r] leave traces of their shape.

Did you know...

Not all fossils are dinosaur bones. Fossilized plants have been found, too, and even leaves with dinosaur bite marks on them!

WHERE IS THE BEST PLACE TO FIND A FOSSIL?

Fossils are only found in a type of crumbly, sandy stone called sedimentary rock. Cliffs and rocky deserts are usually made of sedimentary rock, and fossils are often found in these areas.

Did you know...

At Ghost Ranch in New Mexico, USA, experts found the biggest number of dinosaur fossils ever. Hundreds of small, meat-eating dinosaurs called Coelophysis (see-low-fye-sis) died there, perhaps killed by a volcanic eruption.

WHICH ARE THE BIGGEST DINO FOSSILS?

The biggest fossils are the bones of sauropods (sore-oh-pods) – giant, plant-eating dinosaurs. For instance, a huge forearm was found in Spain measuring 1.78 metres long, the size of an average man! It may have belonged to a super-sized sauropod called Paralititan (par-a-li-ti-tan).

Did you know...

Dinosaurs often leave behind only one or two fossilized bones. Scientists have to try to work out the size of the dinosaur from just these few remains.

WHICH IS THE SMALLEST FOSSIL EVER FOUND?

A neck bone measuring just 7.1 millimetres long, found in England, turned out to be a tiny piece of a small, bird-like dinosaur called Maniraptoran (man-ee-rap-tor-an). Maniraptoran was probably about the size of a small chicken.

Did you know...

Scientists compare the pieces they find to other dinosaurs found around the world, to see if they can match up the size and shape.

WHAT WAS THE FIRST FOSSIL EVER FOUND?

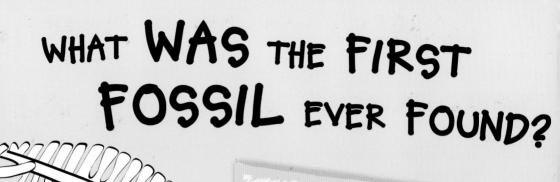

Did you know...

At first, people thought that Megalosaurus walked on all fours, but we now know that it walked on two legs, like Tyrannosaurus rex did.

A hunter called Megalosaurus (meg-al-oh-saw-rus) was the first fossil to be identified as a dinosaur. Parts of it were first discovered in the 1700s, and people at the time thought that it might belong to a giant human. It was finally recognized as a dinosaur in 1824.

WHO NAMED THE FIRST DINOSAUR?

A British fossil expert called William Buckland (born in 1784) was the first person to realize that the Megalosaurus remains were those of a giant, lizard-like creature. He gave it the first-ever dinosaur name.

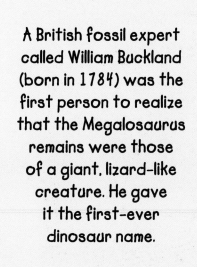

Did you know...

The name 'Megalosaurus' means 'great lizard'.

WHY DO DINOSAURS HAVE LONG NAMES?

Did you know...

A dinosaur's name is often made up of the Latin words for how it looked or behaved. For instance, Oviraptor (oh-vee-rap-tor) means 'egg thief'.

TYRANNOSAURUS REX

Dinosaur names are written in Latin, a very old language first used by the ancient Romans. Scientists use Latin to name all the Earth's creatures. That way, everyone around the world can use the same name.

STRUTHIOMIMUS

WHICH DINOSAUR HAS THE LONGEST NAME?

Micropachycephalosaurus (mike-row-pak-ee-keff-ah-loh-sore-us) has the longest name of any dinosaur. It was a tiny plant-eater, about 17 centimetres tall. Its name means 'tiny thick-headed lizard'.

Did you know...

The word 'dinosaur' comes from the Greek words 'deinos' ('terrible')and 'sauros' ('lizard'). So dinosaur means 'terrible lizard'.

MICROPACHYCEPHALOSAURUS

WHAT HAPPENED TO THE DINOSAURS?

Sixty-five million years ago, many of the dinosaurs died out. Scientists think that the weather on Earth may have changed, so the plants died and there was not enough food for the dinosaurs. This might have happened because large volcanoes erupted, or because an asteroid from space hit the Earth. We may never know for certain.

Did you know...

Small animals, such as mammals and insects, survived when the dinosaurs died out. Perhaps they needed less food than the dinosaurs.

COULD THE DINOSAURS COME BACK?

Did you know...

It is possible that some dinosaurs survived, evolved and are living with us now as birds! What do you think?

In the story Jurassic Park, scientists bring dinosaurs back to life by copying their DNA, chemicals found in the cells of the body. In real life, nobody has found any dinosaur DNA, not yet. If we do find any, the DNA would probably be far too old to use.

QUICK-QUIZ QUESTIONS

1. People once thought dinosaur bones belonged to giant humans. True or false?

2. How long did dinosaurs live on Earth?

3. How big was the wingspan of the biggest prehistoric dragonfly? Was it 35 centimetres, 75 centimetres or 200 centimetres?

4. Who had the sharpest teeth, carnivores or herbivores?

5. Some dinosaurs had feathers. True or false?

6. Were duck-billed dinosaurs called therosaurs or hadrosaurs?

7. What did the world's biggest dinosaurs eat?

8. The biggest dinosaur footprints ever found were 2 metres across. True or false?

9. What is the name of the biggest meat-eating dinosaur found so far, Tyrannosaurus rex or Spinosaurus?

10. Which dinosaur had three, metre-long claws on each forearm?

11. Was Liopleurodon a giant, plant-eating dinosaur or a reptile that swam in the sea?

12. Did Microraptor have curved claws for climbing trees or for swimming?

13. Some plant-eating dinosaurs lived in herds, like cattle do today. True or false?

14. Which dinosaur laid the biggest eggs we know about?

15. Does the dinosaur name 'Maiasaura' mean 'good mother lizard' or 'good baby lizard'?

16. Dinosaurs could not smell each other. True or false?

17. Did dinosaurs only hunt in daylight?

18. Did all dinosaurs have armour?

19. How do scientists work out the size of a dinosaur's eye? Do they measure the eye socket or the eyeball?

20. Did Stegosaurus have plates or spikes along its back?

21. Is a fossil hard or soft?

22. How long was the neck bone of the tiniest dinosaur we know about? Was it 3.1 millimetres, 7.1 millimetres or 15.1 millimetres long?

23. Megalosaurus was the first dinosaur to be named. Does the name mean 'long lizard' or 'great lizard'?

24. Dinosaur names are written in which language?

25. How many years ago did dinosaurs die out?

57

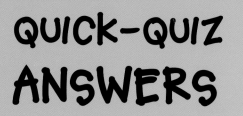

QUICK-QUIZ ANSWERS

1. True.
2. For 165 million years.

3. 75 centimetres.

4. Carnivores (meat-eaters).

5. True.
6. Hadrosaurs.

7. Plants.

8. True.
9. Spinosaurus.

10. Therizinosaurus.
11. A reptile that swam in the sea.

12. For climbing trees.

13. True.

14. Hypselosaurus.

15. Good mother lizard.
16. False, they could smell each other.

17. No, some probably hunted at night.

18. No.
19. They measure the eye socket.

20. Plates.

21. Hard.
22. 7.1 millimetres.

23. Megalosaurus means 'great lizard'.

24. Latin.
25. 65 million years ago.

TRICKY WORDS

ASTEROID
A large piece of rock that hurtles through space. Asteroids sometimes crash into planets.

CARNIVORE
An animal that only eats meat.

COPROLITE
The scientific name for fossilized dinosaur poo.

CREST
A ridge on top of a dinosaur's head, made of horn–like material.

DINOSAUR
A Latin word meaning 'terrible lizard' and the name given to the many different reptiles that lived on land between 230 and 65 million years ago.

DNA
A set of chemicals inside each cell of a living creature.

EVOLUTION
The process by which creatures gradually adapt to their environment and change shape, size and behaviour over millions of years, to make sure they survive.

EXCAVATED
Carefully dug out of the ground.

EXTINCT
When a type of creature dies out and none of its kind are left.

EYE SOCKETS
The bony, round holes in the head of a skeleton, where the eyeballs fit.

FOSSIL
The remains of a plant or an animal preserved in rock.

HADROSAURS
A group of dinosaurs that had mouths shaped like the beak of a duck.

HERBIVORE
A creature that only eats plants.

LATIN
An ancient language used by scientists to name all living things.

MAMMAL
A warm–blooded animal, with hair or fur, that drinks its mother's milk when it is born. Humans are mammals.

MIGRATE

To move from one region or habitat to another — for example, as the seasons change

NIGHT VISION

Eyesight that is adapted to see in the dark. Cats have night vision.

OMNIVORE

A creature that eats both meat and plants.

OVIRAPTOR

A group of bird-like, hunting dinosaurs with feathers.

PALAEONTOLOGIST

Someone who studies dinosaur remains.

PREDATOR

An animal that hunts other animals to eat.

PREHISTORIC

Describes the period of history before our written records began.

PREY

An animal that is hunted by others.

PTEROSAURS

A group of flying reptiles that lived at the same time as the dinosaurs.

REPTILES

A group of animals that have scaly skin and lay eggs.

SAUROPODS

A group of very large dinosaurs that ate plants. Sauropods were the largest land animals that ever lived.

SEDIMENTARY ROCK

A crumbly type of rock formed over millions of years from sand or mud. Fossils are found in sedimentary rock.

WHERE TO FIND STUFF

Wow! What an amazing journey! We hope you had as much fun as we did, and learnt many new things. Who knew there was so much to discover about dinosaurs! Here are some other exciting books in which you'll find more to explore:

The Book Of... How?
The Book Of... What?
The Book Of... Where?
The Book Of... Which?
The Book Of... Who?
The Book Of... Why?
The Book Of... The Human Body

Look out for these great books!
'Who' knows 'what' we'll discover...

See you soon!